TABLE OF CONTENTS

Written by Fr. David M. Knight
© 2010 Saint Meinrad Archabbey
All rights reserved.

ISBN Number 978-0-87029-438-9

Published by Abbey Press
1 Hill Drive
St. Meinrad, IN 47577

Printed in the United States of America

Invitation

This is the fifth booklet in a series of five. The goal of these booklets is to show you a simple—but deep—way to make your religion your *way of life*.

We are suggesting you do this by simply making it your conscious focus in life to *live out your Baptism*.

In essence, the foundation of every spirituality in the Church is Baptism. That is just another way of saying that the foundation and goal of them all is living the "life of grace." Baptism is the sacrament that gave us a share in the divine life of God: the mystery we call "grace."

Baptism immersed us in five mysteries inherent in the life of grace. And explicitly committed us to living them out for the rest of our lives. No spirituality can ignore any one of the five consecrations and commitments of Baptism and be authentic. Every spirituality in the Church, and every particular "way of life," necessarily includes them.

But sometimes they are not made the focus of explicit notice. And sometimes they are not sufficiently explained.

These booklets hope to remedy that and so enrich the spiritual life and spirituality of every person in the Church.

We asked in the four earlier booklets:

What was promised to you at Baptism? Do you experience God's baptismal promises to you as being overwhelmingly fulfilled in your life?

- Do you know that you have "*become Christ*"?
- Are you experiencing your faith as the gift of *divine enlightenment*?
- Do you think of yourself as a *prophet*? Do you experience the "gift of the Holy Spirit"?

- Are you aware that you became a *priest* at Baptism? That you are called to *spousal love* of God? And fruitful ministry? What does that mean?

- And are you fulfilling your side of the bargain? Are you aware of what that is?

We ask now: Are you aware that you are a *king* or *steward* of the kingship of Christ?

What does that mean? What mystery is enfolded in it? What promise does it hold out to you? To what does it commit you?

To answer those questions, we need to look into the mystery of the "Kingdom of God." Should we expect it here or hereafter? Is it something we ourselves are bringing about, or can we just wait for it to happen? What role does this play in the "new evangelization"?

All of this revolves around our baptismal commitment to *stewardship*. Rightly understood, stewardship may be our most total response to God.

> Strive first for the kingdom of God and his righteousness, and all these things will be given to you as well.

> The kingdom of heaven is like treasure hidden in a field, which someone found and hid; then in his joy he goes and sells all that he has and buys that field.[1]

---

[1] See *Matthew* 6:33; 13:44.

The Fifth Promise of Baptism:
Victory

Commitment: Stewardship

"Take courage; I have conquered the world!"
"As Christ was anointed . . . King, so may you live always as a
member of his body."[2]

It strikes me as strange that when my generation was growing up we heard little or nothing about the fundamental theme that characterized the preaching of Jesus: the Kingdom of God.

> Jesus came to Galilee, proclaiming the good news of God, and saying, "The time is fulfilled, and the Kingdom of God has come near; repent, and believe in the good news."[3]

We heard a lot about repenting, but to "repent" only meant to turn away from obvious sins, and it was in order to "get to heaven," not because the "Kingdom of God" had come near.

We were never told that we had been launched by Baptism into the work of bringing about a whole new way of thinking on earth, a whole new set of priorities and values, a whole new standard of behavior that would change everything people did — at home and in school, in church, business, social life, and family.

It was not impressed upon us that we were called to revolutionize our culture and the culture of every society on earth.

And there was no great emphasis or focus put on the promise that this would be accomplished; that the Kingdom would come. This didn't fire up our motivation on a day-to-day basis.

---

[2]*John* 16:33; Rite *of Baptism for Children*, no. 98.
[3]*Mark* 1:14-15. See *also Matthew* 4:23; 9:35; *Luke* 8:1; *Acts* 8:12; 20:25; 28:31.

There also wasn't much emphasis on the "Good News." It was implicit, of course, in everything we learned from the Church, but we weren't really excited about how good our religion was. And we didn't experience it as news. Especially as the news that the "Kingdom of God" was about to come into being.

No wonder the last four popes have been calling for a "new evangelization."

"Proclaiming the good news of the kingdom"

The ministry of Jesus is summarized twice by Matthew in identical words:

Jesus went throughout Galilee, teaching in their synagogues and proclaiming the good news of the kingdom and curing every disease and every sickness among the people.[4]

Whatever people understood or Jesus actually meant by the "Kingdom of God," there is no doubt that it was the headline event of the Good News when he preached it. Jesus said repeatedly that this is what he came to preach: "I must proclaim *the good news of the Kingdom of God* to the other cities also; for I was sent for this purpose."[5]

The Kingdom was the subject of the private instruction he gave to his disciples: "To you it has been given to know the secrets of the Kingdom of heaven, but to them it has not been given." And this continued, even after his resurrection:

After his suffering he presented himself alive to them by many convincing proofs, appearing to them during forty days and speaking about the Kingdom of God.[6]

---

[4]*Matthew* 4:23, repeated word-for-word in 9:35.
[5]*Luke* 4:43. See also *Luke* 8:1; 9:11; 16:16; *Matthew* 4:17; 4:23; and 9:35.
[6]*Matthew* 13:11; *Acts* 1:3.

The Kingdom is what he taught us to pray for: "When you pray, say: 'Father, hallowed be your name. *Your Kingdom come....*'"[7]

The Kingdom was what he specifically promised to his disciples: "Do not be afraid, little flock, for it is your Father's good pleasure to *give you the Kingdom....* and I confer on you, just as my Father has conferred on me, a kingdom, so that you may eat and drink at my table in my Kingdom."[8]

The warnings he gave were against attitudes and behavior that would keep people from entering into the Kingdom: "Not everyone who says to me, 'Lord, Lord,' will enter the Kingdom of heaven, but only the one who does the will of my Father in heaven . . . Truly I tell you, unless you change and become like children, you will never enter the Kingdom of heaven.... It will be hard for a rich person to enter the Kingdom of heaven."[9]

The Kingdom was the reward he promised to those who accepted his message: "The righteous will shine like the sun in the Kingdom of their Father. Let anyone with ears listen!... The Kingdom of heaven is like treasure hidden in a field, which someone found and hid; then in his joy he goes and sells all that he has and buys that field.... Then the king will say to those at his right hand, 'Come, you that are blessed by my Father, *inherit the Kingdom* prepared for you from the foundation of the world'. . . . "[10]

All of us who were anointed at Baptism to share in the mission of Jesus as *Priest, Prophet,* and *King* were promised a place in his Kingdom and given a share in his kingship.

> Peter said, "Look, we have left our homes and followed you."
> Jesus said to them, "Truly I tell you, there is no one who
> has left house or wife or brothers or parents or children,
> for the *sake of the Kingdom of God*, who will not get back

---

[7] *Luke* 11:12.
[8] *Luke* 12:32; 22:29-30; 24:26.
[9] *Matthew* 7:21; 18:3; 19:14, 23-24. See also *Matthew* 21:28-43; 23:13.
[10] *Matthew* 13:43-44, 25:34.

very much more in this age and, in the age to come, eternal life."[11]

Paul wrote to Timothy: "If we endure, we will also reign with him."[12]

And the *Book of Revelation*: "You have made them to be a kingdom and priests serving our God, and they will reign on earth."[13]

Do we really believe that as *stewards of the kingship of Christ* we will "reign on earth"? Did Jesus promise this? Does it motivate anything we do?

Here or hereafter?

Our temptation is to interpret this promise—and everything dealing with the "Kingdom"—as if it referred only to heaven or, at most, to the day when there will be "a new heaven and a new earth," after Jesus returns in glory at the end of the world.[14]

Mahalia Jackson once said, "Some people are so heavenly-minded they are no earthly good." In the same way, the "Kingdom of heaven" or "Kingdom of God" has become for us such an other-worldly concept that it hardly enters into our calculations about life on this planet. We work to "get to heaven," but not to establish the "Kingdom of heaven" on earth. We can be so "other-worldly" in our religion that we don't focus very seriously on what we should be accomplishing during the time of our "stewardship" in this world.

That is why our baptismal consecration to share in the anointing of Jesus as *King* may mean little to us. For the most part we just never think of ourselves as "stewards of his kingship." We are not excited by the announcement that "the Kingdom of God is at hand," because it doesn't seem to promise anything that touches

[11]*Luke* 18:28-30
[12]*2Timothy* 2:12.
[13]*Revelation* 5:10.
[14]*Revelation* 21:1.

our lives here and now. It doesn't motivate us to do much about the conditions of life in our society. The goal we focus on—"getting to heaven"—is not synonymous with realizing the Kingdom of God on this earth. So the proclamation that the "Kingdom of heaven is at hand" is not motivating news to us today.

So have we really heard the "good news"? Have we been authentically "evangelized"?

The proclamation of the Good News is that *Jesus came to establish the Kingdom—here as well as hereafter.* And at Baptism we were consecrated to work for it.

Furthermore, Christ promises us victory.

Jesus came as King

We think of Jesus as "Savior," "Teacher," and "Lord," but very seldom as "King."

In Jesus' own time, however, the role people gave to the "Messiah" was the role of *king*; specifically, "the king who would… bring Israel to its destiny…. The title *Messiah-Christ* meant kingship before it meant anything else; and everything suggests that to most Jews it meant nothing else." Why is it that in our time we seldom think or speak of Jesus as "King," and speak even less frequently about his "Kingdom"?[15]

One of the first things said of Jesus was that he was coming as King. This was the declaration the angel made to Mary before his birth:

You will conceive in your womb and bear a son, and you will name him Jesus. He will be great, and will be called the Son of the Most High, and the *Lord God will give to him the throne of his ancestor David. He will reign over the house of Jacob forever, and of his Kingdom there will be no end.*

---

[15]John McKenzie, *The Power and the Wisdom,* Bruce, 1965, pp. 73, 76.

8

This was the title under which he was first introduced to the Gentiles:

In the time of King Herod, after Jesus was born in Bethlehem of Judea, wise men from the East came to Jerusalem, asking, "Where is the child who has been born king of the Jews? For we observed his star at its rising, and have come to pay him homage."[16]

This was the title under which his future apostle Nathanael recognized him: "Rabbi, you are the Son of God! You are the King of Israel!" Jesus never repudiated the title, although he unequivocally refused to be the *kind* of king people wanted him to be: "When Jesus realized that they were about to come and take him by force to make him king, he withdrew again to the mountain by himself."[17]

This was the significance of his triumphal entry into Jerusalem. He entered as king, although it was to die as a criminal and "so enter into his glory."

The next day the great crowd that had come to the festival heard that Jesus was coming to Jerusalem. So they took branches of palm trees and went out to meet him, shouting, "Hosanna! Blessed is the one who comes in the name of the Lord—the King of Israel!" Jesus found a young donkey and sat on it; as it is written: "Do not be afraid, daughter of Zion. Look, *your king is coming,* sitting on a donkey's colt!"

Some of the Pharisees in the crowd said to him, "Teacher, order your disciples to stop." He answered, "I tell you, if these were silent, the stones would shout out."

His disciples did not understand these things at first; but when Jesus was glorified, then they remembered that these things had been written of him and had been done to him.[18]

---

[16]*Luke* 1:33; *Matthew* 2:1-2.
[17]*John* 1:49; 6:15.
[18]*John* 12:13-16; *Luke* 19:39-40.

When he was delivered up to Pilate, "king" was the title he claimed—although not in the sense Pilate thought it had—and "king" was the title Pilate insisted on giving him:

> Pilate asked him, "So you are a king?" Jesus answered, "You say that I am a king. For this I was born, and for this I came into the world, to testify to the truth. Everyone who belongs to the truth listens to my voice."
>
> Pilate also had an inscription written and put on the cross. It read, "Jesus of Nazareth, the King of the Jews." Then the chief priests of the Jews said to Pilate, "Do not write, 'The King of the Jews,' but, 'This man said, I am King of the Jews.'"
>
> Pilate answered, "What I have written I have written."[19]

This is the title we share from our baptismal anointing as "prophets, priests, and *kings*." So we need to look at what the "kingship" of Jesus should mean to us today, and how we need to be involved in it.

We are "kings in the King"—stewards of his kingship

The Church insists today that a "constitutive element" of the process of evangelization—or "proclaiming the good news of the Kingdom"[20]—is to work for peace and justice *in the world*. This is an explicit fulfillment of our baptismal consecration as "kings." As the stewards of Christ's kingship on earth we commit ourselves to *take responsibility for bringing every area and activity of human life on earth under the life-giving reign of Christ*. We dedicate ourselves to transforming the social structures of this world.[21]

This is the emphatic teaching of the popes who have called for a "new evangelization"—both *of* the Church and *by* the Church—to

---

[19]*John* 18:37; 19:19-22.
[20]For this description of evangelization, see *Matthew* 4:23; 9:35; *Luke* 8:1; *Acts* 8:12.
[21]See Pope Paul VI, *On Evangelization in the Modern World.*

respond to the reality of our times. Over the following pages you will see quoted material interspersed within the text. You may wish to refer to the footnotes for these sources. These many references are offered to you in order to show the major emphasis the Church continues to give to this theme of establishing Christ's Kingdom.[22]

Papal Doctrine

Jesus "first of all proclaims a kingdom, the Kingdom of God." This is "so important that, by comparison, everything else becomes 'the rest,' which is given in addition.[23] Only the Kingdom is absolute and it makes everything else relative."

The proclamation of the Kingdom is, for Christ's followers, a call to *action*. We are dedicated by Baptism to the cause of the Kingdom. There is no time for looking back, even less for "settling into laziness." There is work to be done. We must reject the temptation to reduce Christianity to a "privatized and individualistic spirituality." It is in contradiction to our Baptism to "remain indifferent" to the problems of our times or to be "disinterested in the welfare of our fellow human beings."[24]

---

[22]What follows is taken from Paul VI's Apostolic Exhortation *Evangelization in the Modern World,* promulgated on December 8, 1975, and John Paul II's Apostolic Letter *At the Beginning of the New Millennium,* issued for the close of the Jubilee Year 2000. Most of what is given here is directly quoted from these documents, but instead of cluttering the text with an overwhelming number of quotation marks and references I refer the reader to **Evangelii Nuntiandi,** numbers 8, 15, 20, 23; and to **Novo Millennio Ineunte,** numbers 5, 15, 46-51. These documents also refer repeatedly to the Second Vatican Council's documents, *Dogmatic Constitution on the Church* (**Lumen Gentium**), *Pastoral Constitution on the Church in the Modern World* (**Gaudium et Spes**), and *Decree on the Apostolate of the Laity* (**Apostolicam Actuositatem**). See also the Council's *Declaration on Religious Liberty* (**Dignitatis Humanae**), and *Decree on the Church's Missionary Activity* (**Ad Gentes**).
[23]*Matthew* 6:33.
[24]*Pastoral Constitution on the Church in the Modern World,* **Gaudium et Spes,** no. 34.

Christians know, it is true, that "here we have no lasting city, but we are looking for the city that is to come." Our "citizenship is in heaven, and it is from there that we are expecting a Savior," waiting in "joyful hope for the coming of our Savior, Jesus Christ."[25]

However, this "eschatological tension" that keeps us living with one foot in this world and one foot in the next, in no way implies that we withdraw from "building history." On the contrary, "Christianity is a religion rooted in history!" It was "in the soil of history" that God made a covenant with Israel and prepared humanity for the birth of his Son "in the fullness of time."[26] Christ is the "foundation and center of history… its meaning and ultimate goal." His incarnation is the "pulsating heart of time, the mysterious hour in which the Kingdom of God came to us, indeed took root *in our history*, as the seed destined to become a great tree."[27]

The Kingdom, then, is not just something we will enjoy after death; it is something to be realized in history, in our world, in our time. The Kingdom, in fact, is "the meaning of history and the light of life's journey." Christians find—and make—their way in this world in the light of the Kingdom they are working to establish.

The transformation of cultures

When we say "Kingdom," we are talking about a transformation of society itself. "What matters is to evangelize human *culture* and cultures, not in a purely decorative way, as it were, by applying a thin veneer, but in a vital way, in depth and right to their very roots."[28]

A culture is made up of a whole complex of attitudes, values, priorities, ways of thinking and behaving that have come to be accepted as normal in a particular society. A culture is something

---

[25] *Philippians* 3:20; *Hebrews* 13:14; and see the *Rite of Communion* at Mass.
[26] *Galatians* 4:4.
[27] *See Mark* 1:15, 4:30-32.
[28] *The Church in the Modern World* (**Gaudium et Spes**), no. 53.

people "fit into," something they conform to more than they realize, even when, in one area or another, they see themselves as "non-conformist." We cannot escape the influence of culture. "Culture" is everything we have learned from others in our society, good and bad—from our family, school, church, social circle, professional milieu, and political climate. From parents, siblings, preachers, teachers, friends, and associates. Culture seeps into and gives its taste to everything we are and experience, like rum in a rum cake. We have no idea how we would experience ourselves or any aspect of our lives without the influence of cultural conditioning. We can't even imagine how we would experience the most basic ingredients of our consciousness if we were in some "pure state," unformed and unaffected by culture. Our sense of security and success, competitiveness, defensive instincts, sexuality, relationship with others—all of these have been both formed and deformed by the influence of the culture we grew up in and absorbed. That influence is immeasurable and, in great part, undetectable. For the most part, we just don't know why we feel, think, and act as we spontaneously do.

Establishing the Kingdom is a matter of bringing people to greater *personal freedom* by making them aware of their unexamined cultural attitudes and values, challenging them, offering alternatives for them to accept in conscious, deliberate choice.

The proclamation of the Kingdom "only reaches full development when it is listened to, accepted and assimilated" in *personal choice*. The Kingdom is only authentic when it arouses a genuine, personal adherence "to a program of life, a life henceforth transformed—in a word, adherence to the 'new world,' to the new state of things, to the new manner of being, of living, of living in community, which the Gospel sets in motion."

Respect for what is natural

The Kingdom brings everything to the level of the divine without destroying or distorting any natural human values. This is "not a case of imposing on non-believers a vision based on faith, but of interpreting and defending the values rooted in *the very nature of the human person.*" The work of the Kingdom does no disservice to natural institutions, but is rather a "service to culture, politics, the economy and the family." This is because in God's Kingdom (which is the Kingdom of the Creator as well as of the Redeemer), "the fundamental principles upon which depend the destiny of human beings and the future of civilization will be everywhere respected."

Christian social action

Establishing the Kingdom of God is different from helping the poor. The Church cannot be authentically herself without service to the poor, of course, and to the rich as well, because the love Jesus preached "of its nature opens out into a service that is universal; it inspires in us *a commitment to practical and concrete love for every human being....* No one can be excluded from our love, since through his Incarnation the Son of God has united himself in some fashion with every person." But for Christians there is "a special presence of Christ in the poor," which requires the Church to make a "preferential option" for them.[29]

But helping the poor is not enough. To establish the Kingdom of God we have to address the *causes* of poverty and of all the elements in society that inflict distress and diminishment on human beings. This directs our attention to the Church's well-known and undeniable "contribution to the social question, which has now assumed a global dimension."[30]

Among the "many needs which demand a compassionate response from Christians," the papal documents alert us to "the contradictions of an economic, cultural and technological progress which offers immense possibilities to a fortunate few, while leaving millions of others.... in living conditions far below the minimum demanded by human dignity."

---

[29] *The Church in the Modern World* (**Gaudium et Spes**)
[30] *ibid.*

How can it be, the popes ask, that even today there are still people dying of hunger? Condemned to illiteracy? Lacking the most basic medical care? Without a roof over their heads?

The modern Church is painfully aware of a "scenario of poverty" that is extending beyond traditional forms to confront us with "newer patterns" in which even financially affluent sectors and groups are "threatened by despair at the lack of meaning in their lives, by drug addiction, by fear of abandonment in old age or sickness, by marginalization or social discrimination."

We "cannot remain indifferent":

- to the "*ecological crisis* which is making vast areas of our planet uninhabitable and hostile to humanity";
- to the "*problems of peace*, threatened by the specter of catastrophic wars";
- to resurgent "*contempt for the fundamental human rights* of so many people, especially children."

All of these are the challenge of establishing the Kingdom of God on our earth, in our time, by our efforts aided by the empowering grace of the light and love of God. Today the "tradition of charity" calls for greater resourcefulness. Now is the time for a "new creativity" in love.

This is a call to action. The Christian message risks being distorted and "submerged in the ocean of words which daily engulfs us in today's society of mass communications." But the proclamation of the Gospel, which is certainly a "charity of words," demands for its effectiveness the "charity of works." More than ever before, to stand in prophetic witness before the world, the Church must measure up to Christ's own criterion: "You will know them by their fruits"; that is, by their deeds.[31]

---

[31]See *Matthew* 7:16.

Action to bring about justice and peace on earth is what the popes are calling "the greatest and most effective presentation of the good news of the Kingdom."

"Take courage; I have conquered the world!"

In seeking to establish the "Kingdom of God" on earth, Christians are taking on the task of transforming all the cultures of the world:

- Making business and politics divine in purpose and policies while leaving their natures intact.
- Freeing family and social life to be experienced interaction with God in human intercourse—an experience of God incarnate, indwelling and expressing himself in ourselves and through others.
- Healing our society's unchallenged—even unrecognized—attitudes and behavior that have veered off toward destructiveness and distortion, mediocrity and meaninglessness.
- Establishing the "reign of God" in every area and activity of human life on earth:

An eternal and universal kingdom:
a kingdom of truth and life,
a kingdom of holiness and grace,
a kingdom of justice, love and peace.[32]

David taking on Goliath. Dreaming the impossible dream. This is the scope of the Kingdom:

For the Church, evangelizing means bringing the Good News into all the strata of humanity, and through its influence *transforming humanity from within* and making it new: "Now I am making the whole of creation new."

---

[32]See the *Preface for the Mass of Christ the King.*

Though independent of cultures the Gospel and evangelization are… capable of permeating all [cultures] without becoming subject to any one of them. They have to be regenerated by an encounter with the Gospel.

What this means in practice is "affecting and as it were upsetting, through the power of the Gospel, the human race's criteria of judgment, determining values, points of interest, lines of thought, sources of inspiration and models of life, which are in contrast with the Word of God and the plan of salvation."

This puts special focus on the "lay apostolate."

The proclamation of the Good News through this "new creativity in love"—a culture-challenging love carried out in action—is in a very special way *the specific vocation of the laity*," who are explicitly called and consecrated by Baptism to "seek the Kingdom of God by engaging in temporal affairs and by ordering them according to the plan of God."[33]

A daunting task. But its accomplishment is a promise of our Baptism. We were consecrated "kings in the King" who arrived proclaiming, "The Kingdom of God is at hand." To empower us, Jesus said, *"Take courage; I have conquered the world!"*[34]

We need courage to dedicate ourselves to the transformation of the world. And given the apparent hopelessness of the task, we need divine courage.

And we need to dedicate ourselves without reserve. Totally.

This calls for the total gift of ourselves to God and to the world. Another word for this is total "abandonment." This is both the foundation and the goal of our baptismal consecration as *kings* or

---

[33]See the Second Vatican Council, "Dogmatic Constitution on the Church" (**Lumen Gentium**), no. 31.
[34]*John* 16:33.

stewards of the kingship of Christ. It is, in a very particular way, the laity's path to perfection.

Stewardship, Leadership, and Abandonment

A "steward" is one who manages the property of another. The steward's principal concern is to be "faithful." This fidelity consists in two things: *renunciation* of all private self-interest, and *responsibility* (exercising leadership) in promoting the interests of the owner in every decision about the use and disposition of the owner's goods.

To be a steward of Christ's kingship is to exercise responsible *leadership* in managing everything that comes from Christ, belongs to Christ, or was created for Christ, in such a way that it contributes to the establishment of the Kingdom of God on earth.

This includes everything.

Everything comes from Christ as source. At the beginning of time, "all things in heaven and on earth were created… through him and for him."[35]

Everything belongs to Christ as King. Jesus said before he died: "All things have been handed over to me by my Father."[36]

The true "mystery of God's will," that he "set forth in Christ, as a plan for the fullness of time," is to *bring all things in the heavens and on earth into one under Christ's headship.*"[37]

In Christ, at the end of time, all things in heaven and on earth will be "united," "gathered up," "summed up," "recapitulated," "brought together under a single head." This is Paul's vision of the radiant glory, shrouded in mystery, of the "end time."

---

[35]*Colossians* 1:16.
[36]*Matthew* 11:27.
[37]*Ephesians* 1:10.

The goal of all creation is Jesus Christ himself, the "perfect man," the body of Christ, head and members, all of humanity brought to the fullness of perfection.

The gifts he gave were… for *building up the body of Christ*, until we all become one in faith and in the knowledge of God's Son, and *form that perfect man* who is *Christ come to full stature*.[38]

To be a "faithful steward," then, is to give, to surrender, to abandon all that one has and is to Christ and then to manage in his name and for his Kingdom everything over which we have any control on this earth.

Stewardship is total giving, and total giving is stewardship. By Baptism we "died" to this world in order to live only as the risen body of Christ on earth. We gave up, in the most radical way, everything we have in this world: all our possessions, all societal claims from human relationships, life itself. Then God placed them all in our hands again, not to own, but to manage for him. By Baptism we became "stewards" of all that is under our control. Our preoccupation is to use and manage our time, energies, talents, relationships, and any possessions that are legally ours, in the way that is most according to God's will, the way that will contribute most to the establishment of his Kingdom on earth. Literally, we own nothing. We simply manage what is God's.[39]

This is the foundational reality of our baptismal consecration as *kings* or *stewards* of the kingship of Christ (and of all our baptismal commitments). By this consecration we are committed to *work* for the establishment of God's reign on earth, but the foundation of that commitment is the total abandonment of all that we have and are to God. To be a steward is to have nothing of one's own, but to

---

[38]*Ephesians* 4:11-13.
[39]This is explicit in the Gospel. Jesus says that all who want to follow him must "die" to: •*possessions: Matthew* 19:21-24; *Luke* 14:33; even to such basics as the need for shelter: *Matthew* 8:19-20; •*relationships: Luke* 12:53; 14:26; 18:28-30; *Matthew* 8:21-22; *Mark* 8:38; 10:29-30; •*marriage: Luke* 20:34-35; •*life itself: Matthew* 16:24-25; 18:7-9; *John* 12:25.

manage everything for God. To accept this is to enter into a state of total abandonment to God.

To arrive at this is the fifth promise and purpose of our Baptism.

From surrender to abandonment

If we don't take the comparison too literally, we can compare the *surrender* we make in our ministry as *priests* with the *abandonment* that characterizes our stewardship as *kings*. We may use for a guide a comparison St. Teresa of Avila makes between the spiritual "betrothal" and the "spiritual marriage" in her *Interior Castle*.

Teresa writes that a difference between the spiritual betrothal and the spiritual marriage is that, in the betrothal, union is not constant. It comes and goes. And we can say there is a parallel to this in the difference between surrendering ourselves to let Jesus within us give himself to others through us in *ministry*—which still takes place in individual actions—and abandoning ourselves totally to God and to the Church in stewardship. In ministry, we give ourselves to God and to others in distinct actions. In total abandonment, we simply give over all that we have and are, whole and entire, to be used for God's service.

> The spiritual betrothal is different [from spiritual marriage], for the two [parties] often separate…. Let us say that the union is like the joining of two wax candles to such an extent that the flame coming from them is but one, or that the wick, the flame, and the wax are all one. But afterwards one candle can be easily separated from the other and there are two candles….
>
> In the spiritual marriage the union is like what we have when rain falls from the sky into a river or fount; all is water, for the rain that fell from heaven cannot be divided or separated from the water of the river.[40]

Or like the water mingled with the wine at Mass.

[40] *Interior Castle*, "Seventh Dwelling Place," ch. 2, no. 4.

We surrender in many different acts. But when we abandon ourselves as *stewards* to the work of the Kingdom, there is nothing left to surrender. All is given. Once and for all.

This is expressed in the prayer through which St. Ignatius brings our response to God to its climax in the last meditation of his *Spiritual Exercises*:

> *Take, Lord, and receive all my liberty,*
> *my memory, my understanding, and my entire will—*
> *all that I have and possess.*
> *You have given all to me. To you, Lord, I return it.*
> *All is yours. Dispose of it wholly according to your will. Give me your*
> *love and your grace.*
> *That is enough for me.*[41]

This is the "prayer of stewardship." To say this prayer from the heart is to arrive—on a personal, individual level, at least—at the victory promised in Baptism. It is to enter into the Kingdom by abandoning ourselves totally to the work of establishing the Kingdom for others.

A simple suggestion: One change at a time

A simple way to live out our consecration as *stewards* of the kingship of Christ—simple, but not simplistic—is just to keep trying to change things you see around you that need changing. Little things, big things, whatever is at hand. From picking up a piece of paper on the floor to starting a new political party.

A key word here is "trying."

To be a faithful steward we do not have to *succeed* in what we do. We just have to be faithful in trying.

---

[41] *The Spiritual Exercises,* no. 234. Translation by Fr. George Ganss, S.J., Loyola University Press, 1992.

We can try by ourselves, as individuals. We can try to enlist the support of others. We can try to convince authorities that they should adopt a certain policy for the whole community—or even declare a change of course. We can try to persuade other individuals to do something in a different way. We may not have the authority or the power to bring these changes about. We just have the responsibility to try.

We can always change the way we ourselves do things. Change begins at home.

Responsibility begins with *noticing*. And noticing is a matter of mindset. We notice things we are concerned about, things we think are "our business." If we think something is "not our business," we tend to "keep our nose out of it." We don't pay attention to it.

As *stewards* of the kingship of Christ, we see everything in this world as "our business." We have accepted responsibility for trying to establish the reign of God over every area and activity of human life on earth. We are alert to anything and everything that needs changing. Everything destructive. Everything distorted. Everything that could be better. Everything that could enhance human life on the planet.

We don't invade others' privacy. But we are alert to the effect individual actions have on the community as a whole. Or on the human race. There is profound, mystical truth in the meditation of John Donne:

No man is an island entire of itself; every man is a piece of the continent, a part of the main. If a clod be washed away by the sea, Europe is the less, as well as if a promontory were, as well as if a manor of thy friend's or of thine own were. Any man's death diminishes me, because I am involved in mankind, and therefore never send to know for whom the bell tolls; it tolls for thee. [42]

---

[42]Meditations, XVII, from John Donne, *Devotions Upon Emergent Occasions*, 1624.

This is a charter for stewardship. It is a foundational concept for Christian leadership.

The mystery is the Kingdom of God. The promise is victory. To help bring it about is a "constitutive element" of our way of life.

Then I heard every creature in heaven and on earth and under the earth and in the sea, and all that is in them, singing, "To the one seated on the throne and to the Lamb be blessing and honor and glory and might forever and ever!" [43]

---

[43]Revelation 5

Key points:

- The "headline event" Jesus preached was that the "Kingdom of God" is at hand. This was the "Good News."
- Our temptation is to interpret this promise as if it referred only to heaven or to the end of the world, when Jesus returns in glory.
- Our baptismal consecration to share in the anointing of Jesus as *King* means we are "stewards of his kingship."
- As the stewards of Christ's kingship on earth, we commit ourselves to *take responsibility for bringing every area and activity of human life on earth under the life-giving reign of Christ.* We dedicate ourselves to transforming the cultures and social structures of this world.
- This is the emphatic teaching of the popes who have called for a "new evangelization"—both *of* the Church and *by* the Church—to respond to the reality of our times.
- Action to bring about justice and peace on earth is what the popes are calling "the greatest and most effective presentation of the good news of the Kingdom."
- This is in a very special way "*the specific vocation of the laity,*" who are called and consecrated by Baptism to "seek the Kingdom of God by engaging in temporal affairs and by ordering them according to the plan of God."
- We need courage to dedicate ourselves to the transformation of the world. And given the apparent hopelessness of the task, we need divine courage. This is the divine gift of *hope.*
- The work of the Kingdom calls for the total gift of ourselves to God and to the world. Another word for this is total "abandonment." This is both the foundation and the goal of our baptismal consecration as *kings* or *stewards* of the kingship of Christ.
- A "steward" is one who manages the property of another. The steward's principal concern is to be "faithful." This fidelity consists in two things: *renunciation* of all private self-interest, and *responsibility* (exercising leadership) in promoting the interests of the owner in every decision about the use and disposition of the owner's goods.

- Stewardship is total giving, and total giving is stewardship. By Baptism we "died" to this world in order to live only as the risen body of Christ on earth. We gave up in the most radical way everything we have in this world: all our possessions, all societal claims from human relationships, life itself. Then God placed them all in our hands again, not to own, but to manage for him.
- To be a "faithful steward" is to give, to surrender, to abandon to Christ all that one has and is and then to manage in his name and for his Kingdom everything over which we have any control on this earth.
- To be a steward of Christ's kingship is to exercise responsible *leadership* in such a way that everything contributes to the establishment of the Kingdom of God on earth.

Questions for reflection and discussion:

- What does it mean to you now to work to establish the "Kingdom of God" on earth?
- Do you see changes that need to be made in your own family life? (Don't mention them if they are private). Social life? Business or professional life?
- What motivates you to work for change on earth?
- What gives you hope when the "Kingdom" seems to be a losing proposition?

A suggested key decision:

Begin by just "noticing" what could be improved in your own environment: at home, at work, in your neighborhood, or city.

Try each day to change one thing, no matter how small.